Best of El Salvador

Top Spots to Explore

© 2024 James Anthony Chambers. All rights reserved.

No part of this book may be reproduced, distributed, or transmitted in any form or by any means, including photocopying, recording, or other electronic or mechanical methods, without the prior written permission of the publisher, except in the case of brief quotations embodied in critical reviews and certain other noncommercial uses permitted by copyright law.

This travel guide was written with the assistance of ChatGPT, an AI language model developed by OpenAI, to provide accurate and up-to-date information. The pictures featured on the cover of this book are license-free images sourced from Canva.

Intro 6

San Salvador: The Heartbeat of El Salvador 8

Exploring Mayan Ruins: Joya de Cerén 11

El Tunco: Surfing Paradise on the Pacific 13

Ruta de las Flores: A Floral Journey Through El Salvador 15

Santa Ana: Colonial Charm and Volcanic Wonders 17

Joyful Journeys in Juayúa 20

Cerro Verde National Park: Where Volcanoes Meet Tranquility 23

Lake Coatepeque: Serenity in a Volcanic Crater 26

A Gourmet's Delight: Sampling Pupusas in Olocuilta 29

Hiking Adventures in El Imposible National Park 31

La Libertad: Beyond Surf and Sand 33

Discovering History in Suchitoto 36

Sunsets and Seafood in El Cuco 39

Tazumal: Ancient Maya Pyramid in Chalchuapa 41

Cultural Riches of San Miguel 44

Birdwatching Bliss in Barra de Santiago 47

El Salvador's Coffee Route: A Journey Through Aromas 50

Concepción de Ataco: A Colourful Colonial Gem 53

Rugged Beauty of Montecristo Cloud Forest 56

Santa Tecla: Modern Art and Gastronomy Fusion 59

Playa El Esterón: Secluded Beach Retreat 62

Unveiling Mystery at Cihuatan Archaeological Park 64

The Magic of Metapán 67

Waterfall Wonder: Cascada de Las Golondrinas 69

Piedra de Comandos: A Natural Marvel in Ahuachapán 71

Adventurous Escapes in El Boquerón National Park 73

Chalatenango: Highlands and History 76

Sun, Sand, and Sea Turtles in Playa San Diego 79

Panchimalco: Artisanal Traditions in the Hills 82

Jiquilisco Bay: Mangrove Ecosystem and Wildlife Sanctuary 84

Colonial Splendor of Izalco 87

Ahuachapán: Hot Springs and Healing Waters 90

Indulging in Indigo: Exploring Apaneca's Dyeing Tradition 92

Wildlife Encounters in El Impossible National Park 95

Tacuba: Gateway to the Volcano Route 98

San Vicente: Exploring Caves and Canyons 101

Piedra Sellada: Rock Climbing Haven in Chalatenango 103

Alegria: The Town That Smiles 105

Joyful Journeys in Juayúa 107

El Espino: Beach Bliss and Seafood Delights 109

Afterword 112

Intro

In the heart of Central America lies a gem waiting to be discovered, a land where every corner whispers tales of ancient civilizations, colonial legacies, and natural wonders. Welcome to El Salvador, a country that captivates the soul with its vibrant culture, breathtaking landscapes, and warm-hearted people.

As you embark on this journey through the pages of our guide, prepare to be enthralled by the diversity that awaits you. From the bustling streets of San Salvador, the pulsating rhythm of its markets and the colonial charm of Suchitoto, to the serene beauty of Lake Coatepeque nestled within the embrace of volcanic peaks, each destination promises a unique experience.

But El Salvador is more than just its picturesque landscapes; it is a tapestry woven with threads of history and culture. Explore the ruins of ancient Mayan cities like Joya de Cerén and Tazumal, where the echoes of a bygone era still linger amidst the crumbling stone temples. Wander through the cobblestone streets of colonial towns like Santa Ana and Concepción de Ataco, where brightly painted houses and quaint cafes beckon you to step back in time.

For the adventurous souls, El Salvador offers a playground of natural wonders waiting to be conquered. Hike through lush cloud forests in Montecristo National Park, where the air is alive with the calls of exotic birds and the scent of wild orchids. Dive into the crystal-clear waters off the coast of La Libertad, where vibrant coral reefs teem with life, or catch the perfect wave at surf meccas like El Tunco and El Cuco.

And let us not forget the culinary delights that await you at every turn. Indulge in the national dish of pupusas, delicious corn tortillas stuffed with cheese, beans, and meat, or sample fresh seafood caught straight from the shores of the Pacific Ocean. Wash it all down with a cup of locally grown coffee, renowned for its rich flavor and aroma.

So, dear traveler, whether you seek adventure, culture, or simply a moment of tranquility amidst nature's beauty, El Salvador promises to exceed your expectations at every turn. Join us as we embark on a journey to uncover the best this enchanting country has to offer, one chapter at a time.

San Salvador: The Heartbeat of El Salvador

In the heart of El Salvador, pulsating with life and energy, lies its vibrant capital: San Salvador. This bustling metropolis is not only the political and economic hub of the country but also the cultural epicenter, where past and present seamlessly intertwine to create a tapestry of experiences that will leave you spellbound.

As you navigate the streets of San Salvador, you'll find yourself immersed in a sensory feast, where the sights, sounds, and smells of daily life blend harmoniously. From the lively markets brimming with fresh produce and artisanal crafts to the grand plazas adorned with historical monuments, every corner of the city tells a story of resilience and renewal.

History buffs will delight in exploring the city's rich heritage, from the imposing National Palace, with its elegant neoclassical façade, to the majestic Metropolitan Cathedral, a masterpiece of Spanish colonial architecture. Wander through the streets of the historic downtown area, where colonial-era buildings stand in stark contrast to modern skyscrapers, offering a glimpse into San Salvador's evolution over the centuries.

But San Salvador is more than just a city of monuments and museums; it is a melting pot of cultures, where tradition and innovation collide to create a dynamic culinary scene. Indulge your taste buds in a culinary adventure, sampling traditional Salvadoran dishes like yuca frita, carne asada, and tamales, washed down with a refreshing glass of horchata or tamarind juice.

For those seeking respite from the urban hustle and bustle, San Salvador offers an abundance of green spaces where you can escape into nature without ever leaving the city limits. Take a leisurely stroll through the lush botanical gardens of La Laguna, or hike to the summit of the iconic San Salvador volcano for panoramic views of the city below.

As the sun sets over the horizon, casting a warm glow over the cityscape, San Salvador truly comes alive. Join the locals in El Salvador del Mundo square, where street performers entertain crowds late into the night, or sip cocktails at one of the city's trendy rooftop bars, where you can dance the night away beneath the stars.

In San Salvador, every moment is an opportunity to immerse yourself in the vibrant tapestry of Salvadoran life, where the heartbeat of the country echoes through the streets, inviting you to become a part of its rhythm.

Exploring Mayan Ruins: Joya de Cerén

In the verdant countryside of El Salvador, amidst fields of sugarcane and coffee plantations, lies a hidden treasure waiting to be unearthed: the ancient Mayan ruins of Joya de Cerén. Often referred to as the "Pompeii of the Americas," this archaeological site offers a rare glimpse into the daily life of the Maya civilization, frozen in time for over 1,400 years.

As you step foot onto the sacred grounds of Joya de Cerén, you can't help but feel a sense of reverence for the ancient civilization that once thrived here. Unlike other Mayan ruins, which primarily consist of grand temples and ceremonial complexes, Joya de Cerén offers a glimpse into the everyday lives of its inhabitants, providing invaluable insights into their culture, customs, and beliefs.

Wander through the meticulously preserved ruins, where you'll find the remains of humble thatched-roof dwellings, communal kitchens, and ceremonial structures, all buried beneath layers of volcanic ash following a catastrophic eruption around AD 600. Thanks to this natural disaster, Joya de Cerén offers a rare opportunity to witness an ancient Mayan village frozen in time, offering a window into the past like no other.

As you explore the site, you'll encounter a wealth of archaeological treasures, from intricately carved stone altars and religious artifacts to pottery vessels adorned with intricate designs and hieroglyphic inscriptions. Each artifact tells a story of a bygone era, shedding light on the daily rituals, traditions, and beliefs of the Maya people who once called this place home.

But Joya de Cerén is more than just a testament to the past; it is also a living testament to the resilience of the Salvadoran people, who have worked tirelessly to preserve and protect this invaluable heritage site for future generations to enjoy. Thanks to their efforts, Joya de Cerén has been designated a UNESCO World Heritage Site, ensuring its continued protection and conservation for years to come.

As you stand amidst the ruins of Joya de Cerén, surrounded by the echoes of ancient voices and the whispers of a distant past, you can't help but feel a profound sense of awe and wonder. For here, in this quiet corner of El Salvador, the mysteries of the Maya civilization await to be discovered, inviting you to embark on a journey through time and imagination.

El Tunco: Surfing Paradise on the Pacific

Nestled along the rugged coastline of El Salvador, where the Pacific Ocean meets the golden sands, lies the laid-back surfers' paradise of El Tunco. Renowned for its world-class waves and bohemian atmosphere, this charming coastal town has long been a magnet for wave riders and sun-seekers from around the globe.

As you make your way to El Tunco, the salty breeze tingles your skin and the rhythmic crash of waves fills the air, heralding your arrival to this slice of paradise. Here, time seems to slow down, allowing you to immerse yourself fully in the relaxed pace of beach life.

El Tunco's main drawcard is undoubtedly its legendary surf breaks, which offer something for everyone, from beginners to seasoned pros. Whether you're carving up the waves at Sunzal Point, testing your skills at La Bocana, or catching barrels at El Zonte, you'll find no shortage of adrenaline-pumping thrills in the waves of El Tunco.

But El Tunco is more than just a surfers' playground; it's also a vibrant community brimming with life and culture. Wander through the colourful streets lined with surf shops, beachfront bars, and laid-back cafes, where locals and travellers alike gather to swap stories, share laughs, and soak up the sun-drenched vibes.

When the sun sets over the horizon, El Tunco comes alive with the sound of live music and laughter, as beach bonfires blaze and impromptu drum circles form beneath the stars. Join the festivities and dance the night away with newfound friends, or simply sit back and savour the magic of the moment.

But El Tunco isn't just about surfing and nightlife; it's also a gateway to a world of adventure and exploration. Embark on a boat tour to nearby La Libertad, where you can snorkel with colourful marine life, or hike to the summit of nearby volcanoes for panoramic views of the coastline below.

As you bid farewell to El Tunco, the memories of sun-kissed days and starlit nights will linger in your heart, beckoning you to return time and time again. For in this enchanting corner of El Salvador, where the surf is always up and the vibes are always good, every moment is an invitation to live life to the fullest.

Ruta de las Flores: A Floral Journey Through El Salvador

Nestled amidst the lush highlands of El Salvador, there exists a picturesque route that beckons travellers to embark on a floral journey like no other: the Ruta de las Flores. Aptly named for the vibrant blossoms that line its winding roads, this enchanting route offers a feast for the senses, where every twist and turn reveals a kaleidoscope of colours and fragrances.

As you set out on the Ruta de las Flores, the air is alive with the scent of blooming flowers and the chirping of tropical birds, creating a symphony of nature's finest melodies. Stretching from the quaint town of Sonsonate to the charming village of Ahuachapán, this scenic route winds its way through verdant valleys, cloud-cloaked mountains, and fertile farmland, offering a glimpse into the soul of El Salvador's countryside.

One of the highlights of the Ruta de las Flores is undoubtedly the abundance of colourful blooms that line its path, from delicate orchids and vibrant bougainvillaeas to fragrant jasmine and towering ceibas. Stop at one of the many roadside stalls to admire the handcrafted flower arrangements, or simply bask in the beauty of nature's handiwork as you meander through fields of wildflowers and towering sunflowers.

But the Ruta de las Flores is more than just a scenic drive; it's also a cultural journey through some of El Salvador's most charming towns and villages. Explore the cobblestone streets of Juayúa, where the aroma of freshly brewed coffee mingles with the sound of bustling market vendors, or wander through the colonial-era plazas of Ataco, where vibrant murals and street art adorn every corner.

No journey along the Ruta de las Flores would be complete without indulging in the culinary delights that abound in this fertile region. Sample freshly roasted coffee straight from the source in the coffee-growing town of Apaneca, or treat your taste buds to a feast of traditional Salvadoran dishes like pupusas, tamales, and empanadas, served up with a side of homemade salsa and curtido.

As you wind your way along the Ruta de las Flores, each passing mile brings with it new discoveries and delights, inviting you to slow down and savour the simple pleasures of life. For in this floral paradise, where nature's beauty reigns supreme, every moment is a celebration of the wonders that surround us.

Santa Ana: Colonial Charm and Volcanic Wonders

Nestled in the western highlands of El Salvador, amidst a landscape of rolling hills and lush coffee plantations, lies the historic city of Santa Ana. Steeped in colonial charm and surrounded by majestic volcanic peaks, this enchanting city offers a blend of culture, history, and natural beauty that captivates the hearts of all who visit.

As you arrive in Santa Ana, you're greeted by the sight of elegant colonial-era buildings, their colourful facades standing in stark contrast to the verdant greenery that surrounds them. The city's rich history is palpable as you wander through its cobblestone streets, where every corner reveals a story waiting to be told.

One of the highlights of Santa Ana is undoubtedly its magnificent cathedral, a stunning example of neoclassical architecture that dominates the city's skyline. Step inside to marvel at its soaring vaulted ceilings, intricate stained glass windows, and ornate altars, or climb to the top of its bell tower for panoramic views of the city below.

But Santa Ana's charms extend far beyond its architectural wonders; it is also a gateway to a world of natural beauty and adventure. Just a short drive from the city centre lies the iconic Santa Ana Volcano, the highest peak in El Salvador and a popular hiking destination for outdoor enthusiasts. Embark on the challenging trek to the summit, where you'll be rewarded with breathtaking views of the surrounding countryside and the turquoise waters of Lake Coatepeque shimmering in the distance.

For those seeking a more leisurely escape, Santa Ana offers plenty of opportunities to unwind and soak up the laid-back atmosphere. Relax in one of the city's charming plazas, where fountains trickle and palm trees sway in the breeze, or sip coffee at a sidewalk cafe and watch the world go by.

As the sun sets over the horizon, casting a warm glow over the city, Santa Ana truly comes alive. Join the locals in Parque Libertad, where live music fills the air and street vendors serve up delicious snacks and ice-cold drinks, or explore the bustling night market, where you can shop for handmade crafts and souvenirs to take home.

In Santa Ana, colonial charm and volcanic wonders converge to create an experience that is as enchanting as it is unforgettable. Whether you're exploring its historic streets, scaling its towering peaks, or simply soaking up its vibrant atmosphere, Santa Ana promises to leave a lasting impression on all who visit.

Joyful Journeys in Juayúa

Nestled amidst the emerald-green hills of El Salvador's western highlands, the charming town of Juayúa awaits, ready to enchant travellers with its quaint cobblestone streets, vibrant markets, and rich cultural heritage. Known for its laid-back vibe and warm hospitality, Juayúa offers a haven for those seeking to escape the hustle and bustle of modern life and immerse themselves in the simple pleasures of rural living.

As you meander through the streets of Juayúa, you'll be greeted by the sight of colourful colonial-era buildings adorned with intricate wrought-iron balconies and red-tiled roofs. The air is alive with the aroma of freshly brewed coffee and sizzling street food, inviting you to indulge your senses and savour the flavours of traditional Salvadoran cuisine.

One of the highlights of Juayúa is its bustling weekend food festival, where locals and visitors alike gather to sample an array of delicious dishes prepared by street vendors from across the region. Feast on mouthwatering pupusas, crispy fried plantains, and hearty stews, washed down with a glass of chicha or tamarind juice, as live music fills the air and laughter echoes through the streets.

But Juayúa's charms extend far beyond its culinary delights; it is also a gateway to a world of natural beauty and outdoor adventure. Lace up your hiking boots and embark on a trek through the surrounding hills and coffee plantations, where lush forests teem with exotic wildlife and hidden waterfalls cascade into crystal-clear pools.

For those seeking a more leisurely escape, Juayúa offers plenty of opportunities to unwind and reconnect with nature. Take a leisurely stroll through the town's tranquil botanical garden, where fragrant flowers bloom and butterflies dance on the breeze, or simply relax in one of the many picturesque plazas and soak up the laid-back atmosphere.

As the sun sets over the horizon, casting a warm glow over the town, Juayúa comes alive with the sound of music and laughter. Join the locals in Parque Central, where impromptu dance parties spring up beneath the twinkling stars, or explore the vibrant nightlife scene, where lively bars and cafes offer a taste of Juayúa's vibrant cultural heritage.

In Juayúa, joyful journeys await around every corner, where the warmth of the people and the beauty of the surroundings combine to create an experience that is as unforgettable as it is uplifting. So come, wander the streets of Juayúa, and let the spirit of this charming town capture your heart and soul.

Cerro Verde National Park: Where Volcanoes Meet Tranquility

Nestled in the heart of El Salvador's lush countryside, amidst a tapestry of emerald-green forests and rolling hills, lies the breathtaking Cerro Verde National Park. A sanctuary of tranquility and natural beauty, this enchanting park offers a haven for nature lovers and outdoor enthusiasts alike, where towering volcanoes and pristine crater lakes beckon visitors to explore and discover the wonders of the natural world.

As you venture into Cerro Verde National Park, you'll find yourself surrounded by a symphony of sights and sounds that awaken the senses and stir the soul. Towering above the landscape like ancient sentinels are the majestic peaks of Izalco, Santa Ana, and Cerro Verde, their rugged slopes cloaked in verdant foliage and crowned with billowing clouds. These iconic volcanoes, each with its own unique character and charm, form the centerpiece of the park and provide a dramatic backdrop for your adventures.

But Cerro Verde National Park is more than just a playground for volcano enthusiasts; it is also a haven for biodiversity, where lush forests teem with exotic wildlife and vibrant flora. Embark on a hike through the park's network of trails, where you'll encounter towering trees draped in moss, cascading waterfalls hidden amidst the foliage, and colourful birds flitting through the canopy above.

One of the highlights of Cerro Verde National Park is undoubtedly its trio of stunning crater lakes, nestled within the calderas of Izalco, Santa Ana, and Cerro Verde volcanoes. These pristine bodies of water, known as Laguna Verde, Laguna de Ilamatepeq, and Laguna de Cerro Verde, shimmer like jewels amidst the rugged landscape, inviting visitors to pause and reflect in their tranquil beauty.

For those seeking adventure, Cerro Verde National Park offers plenty of opportunities to get the adrenaline pumping. Embark on a thrilling zipline adventure through the treetops, soar above the canopy on a paragliding excursion, or challenge yourself to conquer the rugged slopes of Santa Ana volcano on a guided hike to the summit.

As the sun sets over the horizon, casting a golden glow over the landscape, Cerro Verde

National Park truly comes alive with the magic of the evening. Gather around a crackling campfire beneath the stars, swap stories with fellow travellers, and marvel at the beauty of the natural world that surrounds you.

In Cerro Verde National Park, where volcanoes meet tranquility, every moment is an invitation to connect with nature, explore new horizons, and embrace the wonders of the world around us. So come, wander the trails, breathe in the fresh mountain air, and let the spirit of Cerro Verde National Park awaken your sense of adventure and wonder.

Lake Coatepeque: Serenity in a Volcanic Crater

Nestled within the ancient caldera of a dormant volcano, surrounded by lush forests and soaring peaks, lies the serene oasis of Lake Coatepeque. A true hidden gem of El Salvador, this pristine volcanic crater lake offers travellers a sanctuary of tranquility and natural beauty, where time seems to stand still amidst the stunning backdrop of the surrounding landscape.

As you approach Lake Coatepeque, you're greeted by the sight of shimmering turquoise waters that stretch out as far as the eye can see, reflecting the azure skies above and the verdant slopes of the surrounding mountains. The air is alive with the sounds of nature, from the gentle lapping of waves against the shore to the chorus of birdsong that fills the air.

Stepping onto the shores of Lake Coatepeque, you're immediately struck by the sense of peace and serenity that pervades the atmosphere. Surrounded by towering cliffs and dense forests, with only the occasional fishing boat gliding silently across the water, it's easy to forget the outside world and lose yourself in the beauty of this natural wonder.

But Lake Coatepeque is more than just a scenic spot for relaxation; it's also a playground for outdoor enthusiasts and adventure seekers. Embark on a kayaking or paddleboarding excursion across the tranquil waters of the lake, exploring hidden coves and secret beaches along the way, or dive beneath the surface to discover the vibrant underwater world that lies beneath.

For those who prefer to stay on dry land, Lake Coatepeque offers plenty of opportunities for hiking, picnicking, and simply soaking up the sun on its sandy shores. Take a leisurely stroll along the lakeside promenade, where you can admire panoramic views of the surrounding countryside and watch the sun sink below the horizon in a blaze of fiery colours.

As the day draws to a close and the sky is painted in hues of pink and gold, Lake Coatepeque takes on a magical quality that is truly unforgettable. Gather around a crackling campfire on the beach, roast marshmallows under the stars, and let the tranquility of this enchanting oasis wash over you like a gentle breeze.

In Lake Coatepeque, serenity reigns supreme, offering travellers a chance to escape the hustle and bustle of everyday life and reconnect with the beauty of the natural world. So come, immerse yourself in the peaceful embrace of this volcanic crater lake, and let its beauty soothe your soul and rejuvenate your spirit.

A Gourmet's Delight: Sampling Pupusas in Olocuilta

Nestled along the sun-drenched shores of El Salvador, in the charming town of Olocuilta, lies a culinary paradise waiting to be discovered: the humble pupusa. A staple of Salvadoran cuisine and a true delight for the senses, pupusas are a savoury treat that encapsulates the essence of the country's rich culinary heritage.

As you wander through the streets of Olocuilta, the aroma of sizzling griddles and melting cheese fills the air, leading you to the countless pupuserias that line the bustling streets. These unassuming eateries, with their simple decor and welcoming atmosphere, are the heart and soul of the town, where locals and travellers alike gather to indulge in the timeless tradition of pupusa-making.

The pupusa itself is a thing of beauty – a thick, handmade corn tortilla stuffed with a tantalizing array of fillings, from gooey cheese and refried beans to savoury pork, chicken, or loroco, a native Salvadoran flower bud. Each bite is a symphony of flavours and textures, with the crisp outer shell giving way to a soft, doughy interior that melts in your mouth.

But the true magic of pupusas lies in their versatility; they can be enjoyed as a hearty snack, a satisfying meal, or even as a late-night treat after a night of dancing and revelry. Whether you prefer them topped with tangy cabbage slaw, drizzled with spicy salsa, or served alongside a piping hot cup of atol de elote, a traditional corn-based beverage, there's no wrong way to enjoy a pupusa in Olocuilta.

For those eager to learn the art of pupusa-making themselves, many pupuserias offer hands-on cooking classes where you can roll up your sleeves and get stuck in. Learn the secrets of preparing the perfect dough, master the art of shaping and stuffing your pupusas, and discover the techniques for achieving that perfect golden brown crust – all under the guidance of skilled local chefs.

As the sun sets over the horizon and the streets of Olocuilta come alive with the buzz of activity, there's no better time to indulge in the culinary delights that this charming town has to offer. Join the locals at a bustling pupuseria, where laughter fills the air and the scent of freshly cooked pupusas wafts through the streets, and immerse yourself in the timeless tradition of pupusa-making in El Salvador.

Hiking Adventures in El Imposible National Park

Nestled in the rugged terrain of El Salvador's coastal mountains, where dense rainforests meet cascading waterfalls and hidden valleys, lies the breathtaking El Imposible National Park. A haven for nature lovers and outdoor enthusiasts, this pristine wilderness offers a playground of hiking adventures waiting to be explored.

As you venture into El Imposible National Park, you'll find yourself immersed in a world of natural beauty and untamed wilderness. Towering trees stretch towards the sky, their lush canopies providing shelter for a rich diversity of flora and fauna, from colourful butterflies and exotic birds to elusive jaguars and playful monkeys.

The park takes its name from the rugged terrain and seemingly impassable terrain that once deterred early settlers from traversing its depths. But don't let the name fool you – while the terrain may be challenging, the rewards of exploring El Imposible are plentiful. Hikers can choose from a network of well-maintained trails that wind their way through the park, offering opportunities to discover hidden waterfalls, crystal-clear streams, and panoramic viewpoints that take your breath away.

One of the most popular hikes in El Imposible National Park is the Sendero de los Quetzales, or Quetzal Trail, named after the elusive bird that calls the park home. This challenging trek takes you deep into the heart of the rainforest, where you'll navigate steep ascents and descents, ford rushing rivers, and scramble over rocky terrain in search of the park's most elusive inhabitants.

For those seeking a more leisurely hike, the Los Enganches Trail offers a gentler alternative, winding its way through lush jungle and past picturesque waterfalls before emerging at the stunning Mirador de los Enganches, where you can enjoy panoramic views of the surrounding landscape.

But no matter which trail you choose, one thing is certain – each step brings you closer to the heart of El Imposible National Park and the wonders that await within. So lace up your hiking boots, pack plenty of water and snacks, and prepare to embark on an adventure you'll never forget in this untamed wilderness of El Salvador.

La Libertad: Beyond Surf and Sand

Nestled along the sun-kissed shores of El Salvador's Pacific coast, the vibrant town of La Libertad beckons travellers with its promise of sun, surf, and sandy beaches. But beyond its reputation as a surfing mecca, La Libertad offers a wealth of experiences and attractions just waiting to be discovered.

As you arrive in La Libertad, you're greeted by the rhythmic crash of waves against the shore and the salty tang of sea breeze in the air. Surfers from around the world flock to its renowned breaks, such as Punta Roca and El Sunzal, where consistent swells and warm waters provide ideal conditions for riders of all levels.

But La Libertad is more than just a playground for surfers; it's also a vibrant fishing town with a rich maritime heritage. Wander down to the bustling fish market, where fishermen haul in their daily catch of fresh seafood, from plump shrimp and succulent lobster to colourful snapper and mahi-mahi. Sample the local delicacies at one of the nearby seafood restaurants, where the catch of the day is grilled to perfection and served up with a side of traditional pupusas.

For those eager to explore beyond the beach, La Libertad offers plenty of opportunities for adventure and exploration. Embark on a boat tour of nearby Los Cóbanos Marine Reserve, where you can snorkel amongst vibrant coral reefs and swim alongside tropical fish, or hike to the summit of nearby volcanoes for panoramic views of the coastline below.

History buffs will delight in exploring the town's colonial-era architecture, from the iconic lighthouse that stands guard over the harbour to the historic Iglesia San José, with its ornate façade and towering bell tower. Take a leisurely stroll through the town's charming streets, stopping to admire the colourful murals and street art that adorn every corner.

As the sun sets over the horizon, casting a warm glow over the town, La Libertad truly comes alive with the sound of laughter and music. Join the locals at one of the beachfront bars or restaurants, where live bands play late into the night and the dance floor is always packed with revellers.

In La Libertad, the possibilities are endless, whether you're seeking adventure, relaxation, or simply a taste of authentic Salvadoran culture. So come, explore beyond the surf and sand, and discover the hidden treasures that await in this vibrant coastal town.

Discovering History in Suchitoto

Nestled amidst the rolling hills of El Salvador's central region, where the tranquil waters of Lake Suchitlán shimmer in the distance, lies the picturesque colonial town of Suchitoto. Steeped in history and charm, this enchanting town offers travellers a glimpse into El Salvador's rich cultural heritage and a chance to step back in time to a bygone era.

As you wander through the cobbled streets of Suchitoto, you can't help but feel transported to another time and place. Colonial-era buildings with their colourful facades and wrought-iron balconies line the streets, while the sound of church bells echoes through the air, reminding you of the town's storied past.

One of the highlights of Suchitoto is undoubtedly its well-preserved historic centre, where centuries-old churches, convents, and mansions offer a window into the town's colonial past. Explore the graceful arches and ornate altars of the Santa Lucía Church, one of the oldest in El Salvador, or stroll through the tranquil courtyard of the Casa de la Cultura, a former convent turned cultural center that now hosts art exhibitions and workshops.

But Suchitoto is more than just a living museum of colonial architecture; it's also a vibrant hub of artistic expression and cultural exchange. Visit one of the town's many art galleries and studios, where local artists showcase their work inspired by the natural beauty and cultural heritage of El Salvador, or attend a traditional dance performance or music concert in one of the town's charming plazas.

For those eager to delve deeper into the town's history, a visit to the Museo de la Ciudad is a must. Housed in a beautifully restored colonial building, the museum offers a comprehensive overview of Suchitoto's past, from its indigenous roots to its colonial heyday and beyond. Browse the exhibits of archaeological artifacts, colonial-era furniture, and folk art, and gain a deeper understanding of the town's rich cultural heritage.

As the sun sets over the rooftops of Suchitoto, casting a warm glow over the town, you can't help but feel a sense of awe and wonder at the beauty and history that surrounds you. Join the locals in one of the town's lively restaurants or cafes, where you can sample traditional Salvadoran dishes like sopa de mondongo or pupusas, washed down with a glass of local rum or artisanal coffee.

In Suchitoto, history comes alive around every corner, inviting you to explore, discover, and immerse yourself in the timeless charm of this colonial gem. So come, wander the streets of Suchitoto, and let the town's rich history and vibrant culture captivate your imagination and steal your heart.

Sunsets and Seafood in El Cuco

Nestled along the pristine coastline of El Salvador's eastern shores, where the Pacific Ocean meets the golden sands, lies the charming beach town of El Cuco. Renowned for its spectacular sunsets and delectable seafood, this hidden gem offers travellers a tranquil retreat amidst the natural beauty of the Salvadoran coast.

As you arrive in El Cuco, you're greeted by the sight of palm-fringed beaches stretching as far as the eye can see, with gentle waves lapping against the shore and the salty breeze carrying the scent of the sea. It's a scene straight out of a postcard, inviting you to kick off your shoes, sink your toes into the sand, and let the stresses of everyday life melt away.

But El Cuco is more than just a beach destination; it's also a paradise for seafood lovers. Head to one of the many beachfront restaurants that line the shore, where you can feast on freshly caught fish, succulent shrimp, and tender octopus, grilled to perfection and served up with a side of traditional Salvadoran accompaniments like rice, beans, and fried plantains.

As the sun begins to dip below the horizon, casting a warm glow over the sea, the sky comes alive with a kaleidoscope of colours – fiery reds, soft pinks, and brilliant oranges that paint the sky in a breathtaking display of natural beauty. Grab a seat at one of the beachside bars or restaurants, sip on a refreshing cocktail, and watch in awe as the sun sinks below the horizon, casting a golden hue over the ocean.

But the magic of El Cuco doesn't end with the sunset; as night falls, the town comes alive with the sound of music and laughter. Join the locals in one of the beachfront bars, where live bands play late into the night and the dance floor is always packed with revellers, or simply relax under the stars and listen to the gentle lapping of the waves against the shore.

In El Cuco, every moment is an invitation to savour the simple pleasures of life – from the breathtaking beauty of a Pacific sunset to the mouthwatering flavours of freshly caught seafood. So come, escape to the shores of El Cuco, and let the tranquillity and natural beauty of this coastal paradise rejuvenate your spirit and soothe your soul.

Tazumal: Ancient Maya Pyramid in Chalchuapa

Nestled amidst the lush green countryside of Chalchuapa in western El Salvador, the ancient Maya pyramid of Tazumal stands as a testament to the ingenuity and craftsmanship of this ancient civilization. Rising proudly from the earth, its weathered stone steps bear witness to centuries of history, inviting travellers to step back in time and explore the mysteries of the past.

As you approach Tazumal, you're immediately struck by the imposing presence of the pyramid, its massive stone blocks reaching towards the sky like a stairway to the heavens. Built over 1,500 years ago by the indigenous Pipil people, Tazumal served as a ceremonial center and hub of political and religious activity for the region.

Climbing to the summit of Tazumal, you're rewarded with panoramic views of the surrounding countryside, where verdant hills roll away into the distance and the scent of tropical flowers fills the air. It's a moment of quiet reflection, as you imagine the bustling city that once thrived here, its streets filled with traders, priests, and worshippers.

But Tazumal is more than just a monument to the past; it's also a window into the lives of the people who built it. Explore the intricate carvings and sculptures that adorn the pyramid's façade, depicting scenes of daily life, religious rituals, and mythical creatures that were central to Maya cosmology. Marvel at the precision with which the stones were cut and fitted together, a testament to the skill and craftsmanship of the Maya builders.

For archaeology enthusiasts, a visit to the nearby museum offers a fascinating insight into the history and significance of Tazumal. Browse the exhibits of ancient artifacts, pottery, and tools unearthed during excavations at the site, and learn about the ongoing efforts to preserve and protect this important cultural heritage.

As the sun sets over the horizon, casting a warm glow over the ancient stones of Tazumal, you can't help but feel a sense of awe and wonder at the timeless beauty and history that surrounds you. It's a moment of connection with the past, a chance to glimpse into the lives of those who came before us and to appreciate the legacy they left behind.

In Tazumal, the echoes of the past reverberate through the ages, inviting travellers to embark on a journey of discovery and exploration. So come, wander the ruins of this ancient Maya pyramid, and let the history and mystery of Tazumal captivate your imagination and ignite your spirit of adventure.

Cultural Riches of San Miguel

Nestled in the heart of eastern El Salvador, amidst rolling hills and fertile valleys, lies the vibrant city of San Miguel. Renowned for its rich cultural heritage and lively atmosphere, San Miguel offers travellers a captivating blend of history, art, and tradition waiting to be discovered.

As you arrive in San Miguel, you're immediately struck by the city's colonial charm and bustling energy. Elegant colonial-era buildings line the streets, their colourful facades adorned with intricate wrought-iron balconies and wooden shutters, while the sounds of street vendors and musicians fill the air, creating a vibrant tapestry of sights and sounds.

One of the highlights of San Miguel is undoubtedly its thriving arts scene. The city is home to a wealth of galleries, studios, and cultural centres, where local artists showcase their work inspired by the natural beauty and cultural heritage of El Salvador. Wander through the cobblestone streets of the historic centre, stopping to admire the vibrant murals and street art that adorn every corner, or visit one of the many galleries that line the bustling Avenida Roosevelt.

But San Miguel's cultural riches extend far beyond its artistic offerings; the city is also a hub of music, dance, and traditional festivities. Visit during one of the city's annual festivals, such as the Fiestas Patronales or the Festival de la Calle San Miguel, and immerse yourself in the sights, sounds, and flavours of Salvadoran culture. From colourful parades and lively street performances to traditional dance competitions and gastronomic delights, there's something for everyone to enjoy.

For those eager to delve deeper into the city's history, a visit to the Museo Regional de Oriente is a must. Housed in a beautifully restored colonial building, the museum offers a comprehensive overview of San Miguel's past, from its indigenous roots to its colonial heyday and beyond. Browse the exhibits of archaeological artifacts, colonial-era furniture, and folk art, and gain a deeper understanding of the city's rich cultural heritage.

As the sun sets over the horizon and the city lights begin to twinkle, San Miguel comes alive with the magic of the evening. Join the locals in one of the city's lively restaurants or bars, where live music fills the air and the aroma of traditional Salvadoran dishes wafts from the kitchen, or simply stroll along the waterfront and soak up the vibrant atmosphere.

In San Miguel, cultural riches abound around every corner, inviting travellers to explore, discover, and immerse themselves in the vibrant tapestry of Salvadoran culture. So come, wander the streets of San Miguel, and let the city's rich history and lively spirit captivate your imagination and steal your heart.

Birdwatching Bliss in Barra de Santiago

Nestled along the serene shores of El Salvador's southern coast, where the waters of the Pacific Ocean meet the tranquil estuary of the Río de Paz, lies the hidden paradise of Barra de Santiago. This pristine coastal enclave, surrounded by mangrove forests and lush wetlands, offers travellers a unique opportunity to immerse themselves in the wonders of nature and discover the incredible diversity of birdlife that calls this area home.

As you arrive in Barra de Santiago, you're immediately struck by the sense of peace and tranquility that pervades the atmosphere. The air is alive with the sounds of nature, from the gentle rustle of palm fronds to the chorus of bird calls that fills the air. It's a scene straight out of a nature documentary, inviting you to slow down, breathe deeply, and connect with the natural world around you.

One of the highlights of Barra de Santiago is undoubtedly its abundance of birdlife. The estuary and surrounding wetlands provide a vital habitat for a wide variety of bird species, from colourful parrots and toucans to elegant herons and majestic birds of prey.

Embark on a guided birdwatching tour along the winding waterways and hidden channels of the estuary, where expert guides will help you spot and identify the many species that call this area home.

But birdwatching in Barra de Santiago is more than just a hobby – it's a deeply immersive experience that offers a glimpse into the intricate web of life that exists within these fragile ecosystems. As you paddle through the mangrove forests and navigate the maze of channels, you'll witness firsthand the delicate balance between predator and prey, hunter and hunted, as birds go about their daily routines of feeding, nesting, and raising their young.

For those seeking a more adventurous experience, Barra de Santiago offers plenty of opportunities for exploration and discovery. Hike through the pristine coastal forests that fringe the estuary, where hidden trails lead to secluded beaches and panoramic viewpoints that offer breathtaking views of the surrounding landscape. Or rent a kayak or paddleboard and explore the estuary at your own pace, paddling through tranquil waters and taking in the sights and sounds of this natural paradise.

As the sun sets over the horizon, casting a warm glow over the estuary and surrounding wetlands, Barra de Santiago takes on a magical quality that is truly unforgettable. Gather with fellow travellers on the beach or at one of the local seafood restaurants, where you can enjoy a delicious meal of fresh-caught fish and seafood while watching the sky turn shades of pink and gold.

In Barra de Santiago, birdwatching bliss awaits around every corner, offering travellers a chance to connect with nature, explore new horizons, and experience the wonders of the natural world in all its glory. So come, embark on a journey of discovery in this hidden paradise, and let the beauty and serenity of Barra de Santiago captivate your senses and nourish your soul.

El Salvador's Coffee Route: A Journey Through Aromas

In the misty highlands of El Salvador's volcanic belt lies a journey through the soul-stirring aromas of one of the world's finest coffees – the Coffee Route. As you traverse this scenic route, winding your way through lush green mountains and fertile valleys, you'll embark on a sensory adventure unlike any other, immersing yourself in the sights, sounds, and, most importantly, the intoxicating aromas of El Salvador's coffee country.

The journey along the Coffee Route takes you through some of the country's most picturesque landscapes, where emerald coffee plantations blanket the hillsides and towering volcanoes loom in the distance. Each bend in the road reveals a new vista of rolling hills dotted with shade-grown coffee trees, their glossy leaves shimmering in the dappled sunlight.

But it's not just the scenery that captivates the senses along the Coffee Route; it's the tantalising aroma of freshly roasted coffee beans that fills the air, drifting from bustling coffee farms and quaint roadside cafes alike. Stop at one of the many fincas, or farms, that line the route, where friendly farmers will welcome you with open arms and invite you to tour their plantations, learn about the coffee-growing process, and sample the fruits of their labour.

As you wander through the rows of coffee trees, shaded by towering canopies of banana plants and towering guava trees, you'll discover the art and science behind the cultivation of this beloved beverage. From the careful selection of the finest arabica beans to the meticulous process of harvesting, drying, and roasting, every step in the journey from tree to cup is infused with the passion and dedication of the people who call this land home.

But the Coffee Route is more than just a journey through the world of coffee; it's also a chance to immerse yourself in the rich cultural heritage of El Salvador's coffee country. Visit the charming colonial town of Ataco, with its cobblestone streets and brightly painted buildings, where local artisans sell handcrafted souvenirs and traditional foods in the bustling market square. Or explore the historic town of Juayúa, famous for its weekly food festival where you can sample a mouthwatering array of local dishes, including coffee-infused delicacies like coffee-rubbed steak and coffee-flavoured desserts.

As the sun sets over the horizon, casting a golden glow over the coffee fields and mist-shrouded mountains, you'll savour the memories of your journey along the Coffee Route – memories that linger long after the last sip of coffee has been enjoyed. In El Salvador's coffee country, every aroma tells a story, every cup a journey, and every moment an invitation to experience the magic of this remarkable land.

Concepción de Ataco: A Colourful Colonial Gem

Nestled amidst the emerald green mountains of El Salvador's Ruta de las Flores, the charming colonial town of Concepción de Ataco beckons travellers with its vibrant streets, colourful facades, and rich cultural heritage. As you wander through the cobblestone streets of this picturesque town, you'll find yourself immersed in a world of colonial charm and timeless beauty.

Concepción de Ataco is a feast for the senses, where every corner reveals a kaleidoscope of colours that dance in the sunlight. Brightly painted buildings line the streets, their facades adorned with intricate murals and colourful designs that tell the story of the town's rich history and cultural heritage. From the cheerful hues of pink, blue, and yellow to the earthy tones of terracotta and ochre, the colours of Concepción de Ataco reflect the warmth and vitality of its people.

But Concepción de Ataco is more than just a pretty face; it's also a hub of artistic expression and creativity. The town is home to a thriving community of artisans, who showcase their work in the many galleries and workshops that line the streets. From vibrant paintings and sculptures to intricately woven textiles and handcrafted pottery, the artistry of Concepción de Ataco is on full display for all to see.

For those eager to delve deeper into the town's history, a visit to the local museum offers a fascinating insight into Concepción de Ataco's colonial past. Housed in a beautifully restored colonial building, the museum features exhibits on the town's indigenous roots, colonial-era architecture, and cultural traditions, providing visitors with a comprehensive overview of the town's rich heritage.

But perhaps the true beauty of Concepción de Ataco lies in its laid-back atmosphere and friendly, welcoming spirit. As you stroll through the streets, you'll encounter locals going about their daily lives – chatting with neighbours on their doorsteps, tending to their gardens, and enjoying leisurely meals at sidewalk cafes. It's a reminder that in Concepción de Ataco, time moves at its own pace, and there's always time to stop and savour the simple pleasures of life.

As the sun sets over the horizon, casting a warm glow over the town and surrounding mountains, Concepción de Ataco takes on a magical quality that is truly unforgettable. Join the locals in one of the town's lively restaurants or bars, where live music fills the air and the aroma of traditional Salvadoran dishes wafts from the kitchen, or simply stroll along the streets and soak up the vibrant atmosphere.

In Concepción de Ataco, colonial charm meets artistic flair, creating a destination that is as enchanting as it is captivating. So come, wander the streets of this colourful colonial gem, and let the beauty and warmth of Concepción de Ataco steal your heart and ignite your spirit of adventure.

Rugged Beauty of Montecristo Cloud Forest

Nestled high in the misty mountains of western El Salvador, the Montecristo Cloud Forest Reserve stands as a testament to the rugged beauty and biodiversity of Central America's most pristine wilderness areas. As you venture into this enchanting forest, you'll find yourself immersed in a world of mist-shrouded trees, tumbling waterfalls, and vibrant wildlife, where every step reveals a new wonder waiting to be discovered.

The Montecristo Cloud Forest Reserve is a haven for nature lovers and outdoor enthusiasts alike, offering a rare opportunity to explore one of the last remaining intact cloud forests in the region. Here, dense vegetation blankets the slopes of the mountains, creating a lush and vibrant ecosystem that is home to an astonishing array of plant and animal species found nowhere else on Earth.

As you hike through the misty trails of the reserve, you'll encounter towering trees draped in moss and ferns, their branches teeming with life. Listen closely, and you'll hear the melodious calls of birds echoing through the forest, from the elusive quetzal and resplendent trogon to the colourful toucan and cheeky monkey. Keep an eye out for elusive mammals like the jaguar and ocelot, as well as a dazzling array of amphibians, reptiles, and insects that call this forest home.

But it's not just the wildlife that makes the Montecristo Cloud Forest Reserve so special; it's also the breathtaking natural beauty that surrounds you at every turn. Stand in awe at the base of towering waterfalls that cascade down sheer rock faces, their cool mists refreshing your skin and invigorating your senses. Or take a moment to pause and admire the panoramic views of the mist-shrouded mountains and lush valleys below, a scene straight out of a fairy tale.

For those seeking a truly immersive experience, the Montecristo Cloud Forest Reserve offers a range of guided tours and educational programs that allow visitors to learn more about the delicate balance of life that exists within this unique ecosystem. Join a knowledgeable guide on a birdwatching excursion, where you'll have the chance to spot rare and endangered species in their natural habitat, or participate in a hands-on conservation project aimed at protecting the forest for future generations.

As the sun sets over the horizon, casting a golden glow over the misty mountains and verdant valleys, you'll feel a sense of peace and tranquility wash over you – a reminder of the timeless beauty and natural wonders that await in the Montecristo Cloud Forest Reserve. So come, immerse yourself in the rugged beauty of this enchanted forest, and let the magic of Montecristo capture your heart and inspire your spirit of adventure.

Santa Tecla: Modern Art and Gastronomy Fusion

Nestled in the vibrant heart of El Salvador's metropolitan area, Santa Tecla stands as a shining beacon of modernity, creativity, and culinary innovation. This dynamic city, with its bustling streets, contemporary art scene, and eclectic gastronomic offerings, offers travellers a tantalising fusion of culture, cuisine, and creativity waiting to be explored.

As you wander through the streets of Santa Tecla, you'll be struck by the city's unmistakable energy and vitality. Modern skyscrapers share space with colonial-era buildings, their facades adorned with colourful murals and street art that reflect the city's rich cultural heritage and artistic spirit. It's a melting pot of old and new, where tradition meets innovation in a harmonious blend that is uniquely Santa Tecla.

One of the highlights of Santa Tecla is undoubtedly its thriving arts scene. The city is home to a wealth of galleries, studios, and cultural centres, where local artists showcase their work in a variety of mediums, from painting and sculpture to photography and multimedia installations. Explore the vibrant art district of La Libertad, where you'll find galleries tucked away in hidden courtyards and alleyways, or visit one of the city's many street art festivals, where artists from around the world come together to create larger-than-life murals that transform the urban landscape.

But Santa Tecla's cultural offerings extend far beyond its art scene; the city is also a culinary hotspot, with a diverse array of restaurants, cafes, and food markets that cater to every palate and preference. From traditional Salvadoran dishes like pupusas and yuca frita to international cuisines from around the world, Santa Tecla's gastronomic scene is a testament to the city's cosmopolitan character and global outlook.

For those eager to delve deeper into the city's culinary delights, a visit to one of Santa Tecla's many food markets is a must. Sample fresh fruits and vegetables from local farmers, indulge in mouthwatering street food like tacos and tamales, or browse the stalls selling artisanal cheeses, cured meats, and gourmet chocolates. And don't forget to wash it all down with a cup of locally roasted coffee or a refreshing craft beer from one of the city's many microbreweries.

As the sun sets over the horizon, casting a warm glow over the cityscape and filling the air with the aroma of sizzling street food and spicy aromas, Santa Tecla comes alive with the buzz of nightlife and the sounds of laughter and conversation. Join the locals in one of the city's trendy bars or cafes, where live music fills the air and the drinks flow freely, or simply stroll along the bustling boulevards and soak up the vibrant atmosphere.

In Santa Tecla, modern art and gastronomy converge in a dazzling display of creativity and innovation, offering travellers a taste of the city's dynamic spirit and cosmopolitan charm. So come, explore the streets of this vibrant metropolis, and let the modern art and gastronomy fusion of Santa Tecla ignite your senses and inspire your spirit of adventure.

Playa El Esterón: Secluded Beach Retreat

Tucked away along the pristine coastline of El Salvador's Pacific shores lies a hidden gem known as Playa El Esterón. Far from the crowds and bustling tourist hotspots, this secluded beach retreat offers travellers a tranquil haven where the rhythm of the waves and the whisper of the sea breeze are the only sounds to be heard.

As you make your way to Playa El Esterón, you'll feel a sense of anticipation building with each passing mile. The journey takes you through sleepy coastal villages and verdant farmland, winding along scenic coastal roads that offer breathtaking views of the shimmering ocean stretching out to the horizon.

Upon arriving at Playa El Esterón, you'll be greeted by a scene of natural beauty that takes your breath away. Miles of golden sands stretch out before you, fringed by swaying palm trees and gently lapping waves that invite you to dip your toes into the crystal-clear waters. It's a picture-perfect paradise, where the stresses of everyday life melt away, and time seems to stand still. But Playa El Esterón is more than just a postcard-worthy beach destination; it's also a haven for outdoor enthusiasts and nature lovers alike. Spend your days basking in the warm tropical sun, swimming in the refreshing waters of the Pacific, or exploring the rocky coves and hidden tide pools that dot the coastline. Keep an eye out for colourful marine life, from tropical fish and sea turtles to playful dolphins and majestic whales that frequent these waters throughout the year. For those seeking a more active adventure, Playa El Esterón offers plenty of opportunities for water sports and outdoor activities. Grab a surfboard and catch some waves along the pristine coastline, or rent a kayak and explore the tranquil estuaries and mangrove forests that line the shore. And don't forget to pack your snorkelling gear – the coral reefs just offshore are teeming with marine life, offering a mesmerizing underwater world waiting to be discovered.

As the sun begins to dip below the horizon, casting a warm glow over the sands and painting the sky in shades of pink and gold, you'll find yourself reluctant to leave the beauty and serenity of Playa El Esterón behind. But as you bid farewell to this secluded beach retreat, you'll carry with you memories of a truly unforgettable experience – a glimpse into the untouched natural beauty of El Salvador's Pacific coast, and a reminder of the peace and tranquility that awaits those who seek it out.

Unveiling Mystery at Cihuatan Archaeological Park

Nestled amidst the lush green countryside of El Salvador's central lowlands lies a hidden treasure waiting to be discovered – the Cihuatan Archaeological Park. Steeped in mystery and shrouded in legend, this ancient site offers travellers a fascinating glimpse into the pre-Columbian history and culture of the region, where the echoes of a bygone era still linger in the air.

As you make your way to Cihuatan, you'll feel a sense of anticipation building with each passing mile. The journey takes you through rolling hills and verdant valleys, where fields of sugarcane and coffee plants stretch out to the horizon. Eventually, you arrive at the entrance to the park, where a pathway leads you through towering trees and dense vegetation, hinting at the wonders that lie beyond.

As you step into the heart of Cihuatan Archaeological Park, you're immediately struck by the grandeur and scale of the ancient ruins that surround you. Spread out over a sprawling expanse of nearly 200 hectares, the site is home to dozens of meticulously preserved structures, including temples, pyramids, and residential complexes, all dating back to the height of the Maya civilization.

Wander through the labyrinthine pathways of the park, where each turn reveals a new marvel waiting to be explored. Admire the intricate carvings and sculptures that adorn the facades of the temples, depicting scenes of myth and legend that offer a glimpse into the beliefs and rituals of the ancient inhabitants. Marvel at the sheer size and scale of the pyramids, which rise majestically from the forest floor like monuments to a forgotten era.

But perhaps the most intriguing aspect of Cihuatan is the mystery that surrounds its origins and purpose. Despite decades of archaeological research, much about the site remains shrouded in mystery, leaving experts and historians to speculate about its significance and function. Some believe that Cihuatan was a sacred ceremonial center, where rituals and ceremonies were performed to honour the gods and ancestors, while others suggest that it may have been a thriving urban hub, bustling with trade and commerce.

For those eager to delve deeper into the history and archaeology of Cihuatan, the park offers a range of guided tours and educational programs that provide insight into the ancient Maya civilization that once thrived here. Join a knowledgeable guide on a walking tour of the ruins, where you'll learn about the history, architecture, and culture of the site, or participate in a hands-on workshop where you can try your hand at traditional Maya crafts and techniques.

As the sun sets over the horizon, casting a warm glow over the ancient ruins and surrounding landscape, you'll feel a sense of awe and wonder at the timeless beauty and mystery of Cihuatan Archaeological Park. It's a journey into the heart of the past, a chance to unravel the secrets of a forgotten civilization, and a reminder of the enduring legacy of the Maya people in El Salvador's history and culture.

The Magic of Metapán

Nestled in the picturesque highlands of El Salvador's Santa Ana department, the town of Metapán exudes a quiet charm and timeless beauty that captivates travellers from near and far. Known as the "City of Prosperity," Metapán offers visitors a glimpse into the rich cultural heritage and natural wonders of this enchanting region.

As you approach Metapán, you'll be greeted by the sight of lush green hills rolling gently into the distance, their slopes dotted with fields of coffee, sugarcane, and tropical fruits. The air is crisp and refreshing, carrying with it the scent of pine trees and wildflowers that blanket the countryside.

Stepping into the heart of Metapán, you'll find yourself immersed in a world of colonial-era architecture and traditional charm. The town's central plaza, adorned with colourful flowers and shaded by towering trees, serves as the beating heart of the community, where locals gather to socialise, relax, and enjoy the simple pleasures of life.

Take a leisurely stroll through the streets of Metapán, where you'll discover a treasure trove of historical landmarks and cultural attractions waiting to be explored. Visit the town's iconic church, with its striking white facade and ornate bell tower, and step inside to admire the intricate wood carvings and religious artwork that adorn the interior. For those interested in learning more about the history and heritage of Metapán, a visit to the local museum is a must. Housed in a beautifully restored colonial building, the museum offers exhibits on the town's indigenous roots, colonial-era history, and modern-day cultural traditions, providing visitors with a comprehensive overview of Metapán's rich and diverse past.

But perhaps the true magic of Metapán lies in its warm and welcoming atmosphere, where visitors are treated like family and hospitality reigns supreme. Join the locals in one of the town's many cafes or restaurants, where you can savour traditional Salvadoran dishes like pupusas, tamales, and empanadas, or sample fresh-brewed coffee from the nearby plantations.

As the sun sets over the horizon, casting a golden glow over the town and surrounding countryside, you'll feel a sense of peace and contentment wash over you – a reminder of the timeless beauty and enduring charm of Metapán. It's a place where the past meets the present, where tradition and modernity coexist in perfect harmony, and where the magic of El Salvador's highlands comes to life in every corner of town.

Waterfall Wonder: Cascada de Las Golondrinas

Nestled deep within the lush green forests of El Salvador's northern region lies a hidden gem known as Cascada de Las Golondrinas, or Swallow Waterfall. Tucked away from the beaten path, this natural wonder offers travellers a breathtaking glimpse into the raw beauty and untamed wilderness of the Salvadoran countryside.

As you make your way to Cascada de Las Golondrinas, you'll find yourself journeying through dense tropical forests, where towering trees and vibrant vegetation create a verdant canopy overhead. The air is alive with the sounds of birdsong and rushing water, hinting at the natural splendour that awaits just beyond the next bend in the trail.

Arriving at the waterfall, you're immediately struck by the sheer power and majesty of nature's handiwork. Cascading from a towering cliff face into a crystal-clear pool below, the waterfall sends up a fine mist that shimmers in the sunlight, creating a dazzling display of rainbows that dance in the air.

Take a moment to pause and admire the beauty of Cascada de Las Golondrinas, as the cool mist caresses your skin and the sound of rushing water fills your ears. It's a scene straight out of a fairy tale, where the magic of nature takes center stage and leaves you spellbound by its beauty.

For the more adventurous souls, Cascada de Las Golondrinas offers plenty of opportunities for exploration and discovery. Follow the rugged trails that wind their way through the surrounding forest, leading you to hidden caves, natural rock formations, and panoramic viewpoints that offer sweeping vistas of the waterfall and the surrounding landscape.

But perhaps the most magical experience of all is taking a refreshing dip in the cool waters of the pool below the waterfall. Let the invigorating spray wash over you as you swim beneath the cascading waters, feeling the stress and worries of everyday life melt away with each passing moment.

As the sun begins to dip below the horizon, casting a warm glow over the forest and waterfall, you'll find yourself reluctant to leave the natural paradise of Cascada de Las Golondrinas behind. But as you bid farewell to this hidden gem, you'll carry with you memories of a truly unforgettable experience – a journey into the heart of nature's beauty and a reminder of the wonders that await those who seek them out in El Salvador's wilderness.

Piedra de Comandos: A Natural Marvel in Ahuachapán

In the rugged highlands of Ahuachapán, amidst the rolling hills and verdant valleys, lies a natural marvel that has captured the imagination of travellers for generations – Piedra de Comandos, or Commandos Rock. This iconic landmark stands as a testament to the geological wonders of El Salvador and offers visitors a glimpse into the ancient forces that have shaped the landscape over millennia.

As you make your way to Piedra de Comandos, you'll find yourself navigating winding mountain roads that offer breathtaking views of the surrounding countryside. The air is crisp and invigorating, carrying with it the scent of pine trees and wildflowers that blanket the hillsides.

Arriving at the site, you're immediately struck by the sheer size and scale of Commandos Rock. Rising majestically from the earth like a sentinel guarding the valley below, the massive rock formation towers over the landscape, its weathered surface bearing witness to centuries of wind and weather erosion.

But it's not just the size of Piedra de Comandos that captivates visitors – it's also the unique geological features that adorn its surface.

Carved by the forces of nature over millions of years, the rock is adorned with intricate patterns and textures that tell the story of its ancient origins.

For those eager to explore further, Piedra de Comandos offers plenty of opportunities for adventure and discovery. Follow the rugged trails that wind their way around the base of the rock, leading you through dense forests and rocky outcrops that offer glimpses of the surrounding landscape.

But perhaps the most magical experience of all is witnessing Piedra de Comandos at sunset, as the fading light casts a warm glow over the rock and surrounding hills, bathing the landscape in a golden hue. It's a scene straight out of a postcard, where the beauty of nature takes center stage and leaves you spellbound by its splendour.

As you bid farewell to Piedra de Comandos and make your way back down the mountain, you'll carry with you memories of a truly unforgettable experience – a journey into the heart of El Salvador's natural beauty and a reminder of the wonders that await those who venture off the beaten path.

Adventurous Escapes in El Boquerón National Park

Nestled amidst the misty peaks of the San Salvador volcano, El Boquerón National Park beckons adventurers and nature enthusiasts alike with promises of rugged trails, sweeping vistas, and adrenaline-fueled escapades. This natural wonderland, just a stone's throw away from the bustling streets of San Salvador, offers visitors a chance to escape the hustle and bustle of city life and immerse themselves in the untamed beauty of El Salvador's wilderness.

As you journey into El Boquerón National Park, you'll find yourself traversing winding mountain roads that snake their way up the slopes of the volcano. The air grows cooler and crisper with each passing mile, carrying with it the scent of pine trees and earthy vegetation that blanket the landscape.

Arriving at the park, you're immediately struck by the sheer grandeur of your surroundings. Towering trees stretch skyward, their branches reaching out to embrace the mist that shrouds the mountain peaks. The calls of birds and the rustle of leaves fill the air, creating a symphony of sounds that echoes through the forest.

For those seeking adventure, El Boquerón National Park offers plenty of opportunities to get the adrenaline pumping. Lace up your hiking boots and tackle the park's network of rugged trails, which wind their way through dense forests, past cascading waterfalls, and up to panoramic viewpoints that offer sweeping vistas of the surrounding countryside.

But perhaps the most iconic feature of El Boquerón National Park is the crater itself – a vast, yawning chasm that stretches out before you like a gaping maw. Take a leisurely stroll along the rim of the crater, where you'll be treated to breathtaking views of the volcanic landscape below, with its steaming fumaroles and bubbling mud pits.

For those with a thirst for knowledge, the park also offers plenty of opportunities to learn about the geology, ecology, and history of the area. Visit the park's visitor center, where you can explore interactive exhibits and displays that shed light on the unique natural features and cultural heritage of El Boquerón National Park.

As the sun begins to dip below the horizon, casting a warm glow over the mountains and valleys below, you'll find yourself reluctant to leave the beauty and tranquility of El Boquerón National Park behind. But as you bid farewell to this natural paradise, you'll carry with you memories of a truly unforgettable adventure – a journey into the heart of El Salvador's wilderness and a reminder of the wonders that await those who dare to explore.

Chalatenango: Highlands and History

Nestled in the northern reaches of El Salvador, where the rugged terrain of the highlands meets the rich tapestry of the country's history, lies the enchanting region of Chalatenango. Here, amidst the rolling hills and verdant valleys, travellers are invited to embark on a journey of discovery, where the past and present intertwine in a captivating blend of culture, heritage, and natural beauty.

As you journey into Chalatenango, you'll find yourself traversing winding mountain roads that offer breathtaking views of the surrounding countryside. The air is crisp and refreshing, carrying with it the scent of pine trees and wildflowers that blanket the hillsides. It's a landscape that seems untouched by time, where the pace of life slows to a leisurely crawl and the stresses of the modern world fade into the distance.

Arriving in Chalatenango, you're immediately struck by the region's rich cultural heritage and historical significance. The town's colonial-era architecture and cobblestone streets harken back to a bygone era, while its bustling markets and vibrant plazas pulse with the energy of daily life. It's a place where tradition and modernity coexist in perfect harmony, offering visitors a glimpse into the heart and soul of El Salvador.

But Chalatenango is not just a place of historical significance – it's also a haven for outdoor enthusiasts and nature lovers alike. The region's rugged terrain and diverse ecosystems offer endless opportunities for exploration and adventure, from hiking and mountain biking to birdwatching and wildlife spotting.

One of the highlights of Chalatenango is undoubtedly its stunning natural beauty. Explore the region's lush cloud forests and hidden waterfalls, where crystal-clear streams cascade down moss-covered rocks and exotic flora and fauna abound. Or embark on a journey to the summit of one of the region's towering peaks, where sweeping vistas of the surrounding countryside await those brave enough to make the climb.

For those interested in delving deeper into the region's history and culture, Chalatenango offers plenty of opportunities to connect with the local community and learn about their traditions and customs.

Visit the region's many museums and cultural centers, where you can explore exhibits on the area's indigenous roots, colonial-era history, and modern-day cultural traditions.

As the sun sets over the horizon, casting a warm glow over the rolling hills and verdant valleys of Chalatenango, you'll find yourself reluctant to leave behind the beauty and tranquility of this enchanting region. But as you bid farewell to Chalatenango, you'll carry with you memories of a truly unforgettable journey – a journey into the heart of El Salvador's highlands and history, where the spirit of adventure and discovery awaits around every corner.

Sun, Sand, and Sea Turtles in Playa San Diego

As the sun rises over the azure waters of the Pacific Ocean, casting a golden hue over the sandy shores, Playa San Diego awakens to another day of tranquility and natural beauty. Nestled along the coastline of El Salvador, this hidden gem offers travellers a perfect blend of sun, sand, and sea turtles, making it a haven for nature lovers and beach enthusiasts alike.

As you make your way to Playa San Diego, you'll find yourself journeying along winding coastal roads that offer glimpses of the shimmering ocean and swaying palm trees. The air is filled with the salty scent of the sea, invigorating your senses and igniting a sense of anticipation for the adventures that lie ahead.

Arriving at Playa San Diego, you're greeted by a scene straight out of a postcard – pristine white sands stretching as far as the eye can see, gently lapped by the turquoise waves of the Pacific. It's a picture-perfect paradise, where the stresses of everyday life melt away and time seems to stand still.

But Playa San Diego is more than just a beautiful beach destination – it's also a vital nesting ground for endangered sea turtles. From November to February, these majestic creatures return to the shores of Playa San Diego to lay their eggs, creating a spectacle that is as awe-inspiring as it is heartwarming.

For those lucky enough to visit during nesting season, witnessing the sight of a sea turtle laying her eggs is a once-in-a-lifetime experience. Watch in wonder as these ancient creatures emerge from the surf under the cover of darkness, guided by instinct to return to the very beach where they were born.

But the magic of Playa San Diego doesn't end with the sea turtles – it extends to the countless activities and adventures that await visitors on land and sea. Spend your days soaking up the sun on the beach, swimming in the warm waters of the Pacific, or exploring the nearby mangrove forests and tidal pools.

For the more adventurous souls, Playa San Diego offers plenty of opportunities for water sports and outdoor activities. Grab a surfboard and catch some waves along the pristine coastline, or rent a kayak and paddle out to explore the hidden coves and rocky outcrops that line the shore.

As the sun begins to set over the horizon, casting a warm glow over the beach and painting the sky in shades of pink and gold, you'll find yourself reluctant to leave the beauty and tranquility of Playa San Diego behind. But as you bid farewell to this idyllic paradise, you'll carry with you memories of a truly unforgettable experience – a journey into the heart of El Salvador's coastal beauty and a reminder of the wonders that await those who seek them out.

Panchimalco: Artisanal Traditions in the Hills

Nestled amidst the rolling hills of El Salvador's countryside lies the charming town of Panchimalco, a hidden gem renowned for its vibrant artisanal traditions and rich cultural heritage. As you wind your way through the narrow cobblestone streets and pastel-coloured adobe houses, you'll feel as though you've stepped back in time to a bygone era where time moves at a slower pace and craftsmanship reigns supreme.

Panchimalco is perhaps best known for its long-standing tradition of pottery making, which dates back centuries to the time of the indigenous Pipil people who once inhabited the region. Today, the town's skilled artisans continue to produce exquisite pottery using traditional techniques passed down through generations, creating everything from intricately painted vases and bowls to decorative figurines and ceremonial objects.

But pottery is just one aspect of Panchimalco's artisanal heritage. The town is also famous for its vibrant textiles, woven by hand using techniques that have remained unchanged for centuries. Step into one of Panchimalco's many workshops and you'll find artisans hard at work, spinning yarn, dyeing fabrics, and weaving intricate patterns that reflect the town's rich cultural tapestry.

Wandering through the streets of Panchimalco, you'll encounter a wealth of artisanal treasures at every turn. Visit the town's bustling markets, where vendors proudly display their wares – colourful textiles, handcrafted ceramics, intricately embroidered clothing, and more – offering visitors a chance to take home a piece of Panchimalco's vibrant culture.

But perhaps the true magic of Panchimalco lies not just in its artisanal traditions, but in the warmth and hospitality of its people. Take the time to chat with the locals, who are always eager to share their stories and traditions with visitors. Visit one of the town's many family-run eateries and you'll be treated to a feast of traditional Salvadoran cuisine, lovingly prepared using recipes passed down through generations.

As the sun begins to dip below the horizon, casting a warm glow over the hills of Panchimalco, you'll find yourself reluctant to leave behind the charm and beauty of this enchanting town. But as you bid farewell to Panchimalco, you'll carry with you memories of a truly unforgettable experience – a journey into the heart of El Salvador's artisanal traditions and a reminder of the enduring beauty of craftsmanship and culture.

Jiquilisco Bay: Mangrove Ecosystem and Wildlife Sanctuary

Nestled along the southern coast of El Salvador lies the breathtaking Jiquilisco Bay, a natural sanctuary where mangrove forests, pristine beaches, and vibrant wildlife converge in a harmonious symphony of biodiversity. As you embark on a journey to explore this hidden gem, you'll find yourself immersed in a world of natural wonders and ecological marvels that captivate the senses and ignite the spirit of adventure.

Jiquilisco Bay is perhaps best known for its extensive mangrove ecosystem, which plays a vital role in supporting the region's rich biodiversity and providing a sanctuary for countless species of plants and animals. As you glide through the labyrinthine channels of the mangrove forests, you'll marvel at the intricate root systems that rise from the water, providing refuge for juvenile fish, nesting birds, and a myriad of other aquatic creatures.

But Jiquilisco Bay is not just a haven for mangroves – it's also a paradise for wildlife enthusiasts and birdwatchers. The bay is home to an impressive array of bird species, including herons, egrets, kingfishers, and the iconic roseate spoonbill, which can often be spotted wading through the shallow waters in search of food. Keep your eyes peeled for elusive species like the mangrove warbler and the black-crowned night heron, whose distinctive calls echo through the forest.

For those eager to explore further, Jiquilisco Bay offers plenty of opportunities for adventure and discovery. Take a guided boat tour through the mangrove forests, where knowledgeable local guides will introduce you to the region's diverse flora and fauna and share insights into the delicate balance of this unique ecosystem. Or venture out on foot to explore the bay's pristine beaches and secluded coves, where you can swim, snorkel, or simply soak up the sun in peace and tranquility.

But perhaps the true magic of Jiquilisco Bay lies in its profound sense of serenity and solitude. As you paddle through the tranquil waters of the bay, surrounded by the sights and sounds of nature, you'll feel a deep connection to the natural world and a profound appreciation for the beauty and diversity of life that thrives within it.

As the sun begins to set over the horizon, casting a warm glow over the bay and painting the sky in shades of pink and gold, you'll find yourself reluctant to leave behind the peace and tranquility of Jiquilisco Bay. But as you bid farewell to this magical sanctuary, you'll carry with you memories of a truly unforgettable experience – a journey into the heart of El Salvador's natural beauty and a reminder of the importance of preserving and protecting our planet's precious ecosystems for generations to come.

Colonial Splendor of Izalco

Nestled in the shadow of the imposing Izalco Volcano, the town of Izalco exudes an air of colonial splendor that harks back to a bygone era of Spanish influence and indigenous heritage. Stepping into Izalco is like stepping back in time, where cobblestone streets wind their way past centuries-old buildings adorned with intricately carved wooden balconies and colourful facades, each telling a story of the town's rich history and cultural heritage.

Founded in the 16th century by Spanish conquistadors, Izalco quickly became a thriving hub of commerce and culture, thanks in part to its strategic location along the ancient trade routes that crisscrossed the region. The town's prosperity was further enhanced by the fertile volcanic soils that surrounded it, which made it an ideal location for agriculture and farming.

Today, Izalco's colonial charm remains largely intact, with many of its historic buildings and landmarks lovingly preserved for future generations to enjoy. Take a stroll through the town's central plaza, where you'll find the iconic Church of San José, a stunning example of Spanish colonial architecture with its whitewashed walls and ornate bell tower.

But perhaps the most striking feature of Izalco is its location at the foot of the mighty Izalco Volcano, which looms large over the town like a silent sentinel. Known as the "Lighthouse of the Pacific" due to its frequent eruptions in the past, the volcano is now dormant, providing a dramatic backdrop to the town's picturesque streets and squares.

For those eager to delve deeper into Izalco's history and culture, the town offers plenty of opportunities for exploration and discovery. Visit the Museo Izalco, housed in a beautifully restored colonial-era building, where you can learn about the town's indigenous roots, colonial past, and modern-day traditions through a collection of artifacts, exhibits, and interactive displays.

But perhaps the true magic of Izalco lies not just in its historic buildings and landmarks, but in the warmth and hospitality of its people. Take the time to chat with the locals, who are always eager to share their stories and traditions with visitors. Sample the delicious local cuisine, which blends Spanish and indigenous flavours to create dishes that are as vibrant and diverse as the town itself.

As the sun begins to set over the horizon, casting a warm glow over the rooftops of Izalco, you'll find yourself reluctant to leave behind the colonial splendor of this enchanting town. But as you bid farewell to Izalco, you'll carry with you memories of a truly unforgettable experience – a journey into the heart of El Salvador's colonial past and a reminder of the enduring beauty of its cultural heritage.

Ahuachapán: Hot Springs and Healing Waters

Nestled in the lush hills of western El Salvador, Ahuachapán beckons travellers with promises of rejuvenation and relaxation amidst its natural hot springs and healing waters. This charming town, known as the "City of Flowers," boasts a rich cultural heritage and a tranquil atmosphere that invites visitors to unwind and recharge in its serene surroundings.

As you journey into Ahuachapán, you'll be greeted by stunning vistas of rolling hills and verdant valleys dotted with coffee plantations and sugar cane fields. The air is crisp and invigorating, carrying with it the scent of tropical blooms and the soothing sound of flowing water.

Arriving in Ahuachapán, you'll find yourself drawn to the town's main attraction – its natural hot springs. Fed by underground thermal springs, these mineral-rich waters are renowned for their therapeutic properties and have been revered for centuries for their healing benefits. Immerse yourself in the warm embrace of the hot springs and feel your cares melt away as the soothing waters work their magic on your body and soul.

But Ahuachapán is not just a destination for relaxation – it's also a haven for nature lovers and outdoor enthusiasts. Explore the town's surrounding countryside on foot or by bike, where you'll discover hidden waterfalls, lush forests, and panoramic viewpoints that offer sweeping vistas of the surrounding landscape.

For those interested in delving deeper into Ahuachapán's cultural heritage, the town offers plenty of opportunities for exploration and discovery. Visit the historic downtown area, where you'll find colonial-era architecture, bustling markets, and quaint cafes serving up delicious local cuisine.

But perhaps the true magic of Ahuachapán lies in its sense of tranquility and serenity. Take the time to slow down and savor the simple pleasures of life – a leisurely stroll through the town's charming streets, a dip in the hot springs, or a quiet moment spent admiring the natural beauty that surrounds you.

As the sun sets over the horizon, casting a warm glow over the hills of Ahuachapán, you'll find yourself reluctant to leave behind the peace and tranquility of this enchanting town. But as you bid farewell to Ahuachapán, you'll carry with you memories of a truly rejuvenating experience – a journey into the heart of El Salvador's natural beauty and a reminder of the healing power of nature.

Indulging in Indigo: Exploring Apaneca's Dyeing Tradition

Nestled amidst the misty mountains of El Salvador's western highlands, the charming town of Apaneca beckons travellers with promises of a vibrant cultural tradition – the art of indigo dyeing. Stepping into Apaneca is like stepping into a living canvas, where the ancient craft of dyeing fabric with indigo has been preserved and celebrated for generations.

As you journey into Apaneca, you'll find yourself surrounded by lush coffee plantations and picturesque landscapes that seem to stretch endlessly towards the horizon. The air is cool and refreshing, carrying with it the earthy scent of coffee beans mingled with the sweet fragrance of tropical flowers.

Arriving in Apaneca, you'll be immediately struck by the town's vibrant atmosphere and colourful streets adorned with brightly painted buildings and traditional murals. But it's the town's rich indigo dyeing tradition that truly sets it apart as a must-visit destination for travellers seeking a deeper connection to El Salvador's cultural heritage.

Indigo dyeing has been practiced in Apaneca for centuries, dating back to pre-Columbian times when indigenous communities used the natural dye to colour their textiles and garments. Today, the tradition lives on in the hands of skilled artisans who continue to produce stunning indigo-dyed fabrics using techniques passed down through generations.

Wander through the streets of Apaneca and you'll encounter numerous workshops and studios where local artisans practice their craft, transforming plain cotton fabrics into works of art using the age-old process of indigo dyeing. Watch as they carefully mix the indigo dye using natural ingredients, dip the fabric into the dye bath, and hang it out to dry in the sun, where it magically transforms from pale blue to deep indigo before your eyes.

But indigo dyeing in Apaneca is more than just a craft – it's a way of life deeply rooted in the town's cultural identity. Visit one of the many artisanal cooperatives in town, where you can learn about the history and significance of indigo dyeing in El Salvador and even try your hand at creating your own indigo-dyed masterpiece under the guidance of a skilled artisan.

As the sun sets over the mountains, casting a warm glow over the streets of Apaneca, you'll find yourself immersed in the beauty and wonder of this enchanting town. But as you bid farewell to Apaneca, you'll carry with you memories of a truly immersive cultural experience – a journey into the heart of El Salvador's indigo dyeing tradition and a deeper appreciation for the rich tapestry of its cultural heritage.

Wildlife Encounters in El Imposible National Park

Nestled in the rugged terrain of western El Salvador, El Imposible National Park stands as a testament to the country's commitment to preserving its natural heritage. Spanning over 14,000 hectares of pristine wilderness, this protected area is a haven for biodiversity, boasting a rich variety of flora and fauna that captivates the imagination and delights the senses of every visitor who ventures into its depths.

As you embark on a journey into El Imposible National Park, you'll find yourself surrounded by towering mountains, dense forests, and cascading waterfalls that seem to defy gravity. The air is alive with the chirping of birds and the rustling of leaves, creating a symphony of sounds that envelops you in the magic of the wilderness.

One of the park's greatest draws is its incredible diversity of wildlife, which includes over 500 species of birds, 400 species of butterflies, and countless mammals, reptiles, and amphibians. Keep your eyes peeled as you explore the park's network of hiking trails, and you may be lucky enough to spot elusive creatures such as the resplendent quetzal, the endangered Central American spider monkey, or the elusive jaguarundi.

But it's not just the big-ticket animals that call El Imposible home – the park is also teeming with life on a smaller scale. Marvel at the intricate patterns of a tarantula's web, or watch in awe as a kaleidoscope of butterflies flutters by in a riot of colour. Take a moment to pause and listen to the symphony of frogs that serenade the night, or marvel at the industriousness of leaf-cutter ants as they march in perfect formation along the forest floor.

For those eager to delve deeper into the park's natural wonders, El Imposible offers plenty of opportunities for exploration and discovery. Follow one of the park's many hiking trails, which range from gentle strolls through the forest to challenging treks that lead to panoramic viewpoints and hidden waterfalls. Join a guided nature walk led by knowledgeable park rangers, who will introduce you to the park's diverse ecosystems and share insights into the delicate balance of life that exists within them.

But perhaps the true magic of El Imposible National Park lies not just in its stunning scenery and incredible wildlife, but in the sense of awe and wonder that it inspires in all who visit. As you wander through its ancient forests and rugged landscapes, you'll find yourself humbled by the sheer power and beauty of nature, and grateful for the opportunity to experience it in all its untamed glory.

Tacuba: Gateway to the Volcano Route

Nestled amidst the misty highlands of western El Salvador, Tacuba serves as the picturesque gateway to the famed Volcano Route, beckoning adventurers with promises of awe-inspiring landscapes and thrilling outdoor pursuits. As you venture into this charming town, you'll find yourself surrounded by verdant coffee plantations, rugged mountains, and a sense of excitement that hangs in the air like a lingering mist.

Tacuba is perhaps best known as the starting point for the Volcano Route, a scenic journey that winds its way through some of El Salvador's most breathtaking natural wonders. From here, travellers set out to explore the towering peaks of the Izalco, Santa Ana, and Cerro Verde volcanoes, each offering its own unique blend of beauty and adventure.

But Tacuba itself is not to be overlooked – this quaint town is steeped in history and culture, with charming cobblestone streets lined with colonial-era buildings and colourful murals that tell the story of its past. Visit the town's central plaza, where you'll find the iconic Church of San Francisco, a stunning example of Spanish colonial architecture with its whitewashed walls and ornate bell tower.

As you wander through Tacuba's streets, you'll encounter friendly locals going about their daily lives, selling fresh produce at the market or chatting over coffee at a roadside cafe. Take the time to stop and chat with them, and you'll be rewarded with stories of the town's rich heritage and traditions, as well as insider tips on the best places to explore in the surrounding area.

For those eager to embark on the Volcano Route, Tacuba offers plenty of opportunities for adventure and discovery. Join a guided tour to hike to the summit of the Santa Ana volcano, where you'll be rewarded with sweeping views of the surrounding countryside and the shimmering waters of Lake Coatepeque below. Or venture into the Cerro Verde National Park, where you can explore lush cloud forests, shimmering crater lakes, and dramatic volcanic landscapes that seem to stretch endlessly towards the horizon.

But perhaps the true magic of Tacuba lies in its sense of anticipation – the feeling of embarking on a journey into the unknown, where every twist and turn of the road promises new discoveries and unforgettable experiences. As you bid farewell to this charming town and set out on the Volcano Route, you'll carry with you memories of Tacuba's warm hospitality and the excitement of the adventures that lie ahead.

San Vicente: Exploring Caves and Canyons

Nestled amidst the rolling hills of central El Salvador, San Vicente offers travellers a gateway to a world of natural wonders waiting to be explored. While often overshadowed by its more well-known counterparts, this vibrant town is a hidden gem for adventurers seeking to delve into the depths of caves and canyons.

As you venture into San Vicente, you'll find yourself surrounded by a landscape of rugged beauty, where verdant hillsides give way to towering cliffs and hidden valleys. The air is filled with the sounds of rushing water and birdsong, creating a sense of tranquility that belies the excitement that awaits.

San Vicente's main draw lies in its network of caves and canyons, which offer endless opportunities for exploration and adventure. Head to the nearby El Tránsito Cave, where you can descend into the depths of the earth and marvel at the otherworldly formations that adorn its walls. Guided tours are available for those seeking a more immersive experience, with knowledgeable guides leading you through labyrinthine passages and pointing out hidden treasures along the way.

For adrenaline junkies, San Vicente is also home to some of El Salvador's most thrilling canyoning experiences. Strap on your harness and rappel down sheer cliffs, plunge into crystal-clear pools, and navigate your way through narrow gorges carved by centuries of flowing water. It's an exhilarating way to get up close and personal with the natural beauty of the region, and an experience you won't soon forget.

But San Vicente isn't just about adrenaline-pumping adventures – it's also a place of serenity and natural beauty. Take a leisurely hike through the surrounding hillsides, where you'll encounter cascading waterfalls, lush forests, and panoramic viewpoints that offer sweeping vistas of the surrounding countryside. Pack a picnic and spend the day soaking up the sun and enjoying the sights and sounds of nature all around you.

As the sun sets over San Vicente, casting a warm glow over the rugged landscape, you'll find yourself reluctant to leave behind the magic of this enchanting town. But as you bid farewell to San Vicente, you'll carry with you memories of thrilling adventures, breathtaking scenery, and the sense of wonder that comes from exploring the hidden treasures of El Salvador's natural world.

Piedra Sellada: Rock Climbing Haven in Chalatenango

Nestled amidst the rugged landscapes of Chalatenango, Piedra Sellada emerges as a haven for rock climbing enthusiasts, beckoning adventurers with its towering cliffs and adrenaline-pumping routes. This hidden gem offers a thrilling escape into the heart of El Salvador's natural beauty, where climbers can test their skills against the elements while surrounded by breathtaking scenery.

As you venture into Piedra Sellada, you'll be greeted by the sight of imposing rock formations that rise majestically from the earth, their sheer faces challenging climbers to conquer their heights. The air is alive with the sounds of climbers' chatter and the clinking of gear, creating a sense of camaraderie and excitement that permeates the atmosphere.

Piedra Sellada boasts a wide range of climbing routes suitable for climbers of all levels, from beginners looking to hone their skills to seasoned pros seeking a new challenge. The rock here is renowned for its quality and variety, offering everything from slab climbs and crack routes to overhangs and boulder problems, ensuring that every climber finds something to suit their tastes and abilities.

But Piedra Sellada is more than just a playground for climbers – it's also a place of natural beauty and serenity. As you scale the cliffs, you'll be treated to sweeping views of the surrounding countryside, with lush forests, rolling hills, and distant mountains stretching as far as the eye can see. Take a moment to pause and admire the beauty of your surroundings, and you'll be rewarded with a sense of peace and connection to the natural world around you.

For those seeking a more immersive climbing experience, guided tours and lessons are available, led by experienced local guides who know the terrain like the back of their hand. They'll help you navigate the routes safely and efficiently, sharing their knowledge and expertise to ensure you get the most out of your climbing adventure.

As the sun sets over Piedra Sellada, casting a warm glow over the rugged cliffs and valleys below, you'll find yourself reluctant to leave behind the magic of this rock climbing paradise. But as you bid farewell to Piedra Sellada, you'll carry with you memories of thrilling climbs, stunning scenery, and the sense of accomplishment that comes from conquering new heights in the heart of El Salvador's wilderness.

Alegria: The Town That Smiles

Nestled amidst the rolling hills of Usulután, Alegria stands as a testament to the resilience and warmth of the Salvadoran spirit. Aptly named "The Town That Smiles," Alegria welcomes visitors with open arms and a contagious sense of joy that permeates every corner of its cobblestone streets.

As you approach Alegria, you'll be struck by the town's vibrant energy and colourful facades, which seem to radiate happiness and positivity. The air is filled with the sound of laughter and music, and the aroma of freshly brewed coffee drifts tantalisingly from local cafes, inviting you to pause and savour the moment.

Alegria's charm lies not only in its outward beauty but also in the warmth and hospitality of its people. Take a stroll through the town's bustling market, where vendors sell an array of fresh produce, handmade crafts, and traditional foods, and you'll be greeted with smiles and friendly conversation at every turn. Stop by one of the local eateries and sample the town's famous pupusas, a delicious Salvadoran dish made from thick corn tortillas stuffed with cheese, beans, and meat – a true taste of Alegria's culinary delights.

But perhaps the true magic of Alegria lies in its stunning natural surroundings. Perched on the edge of the Tecapa volcano, the town offers breathtaking views of lush forests, rolling hills, and shimmering lakes that stretch as far as the eye can see. Embark on a hike to the summit of the volcano, where you'll be rewarded with panoramic vistas of the surrounding countryside and the opportunity to witness a spectacular sunrise or sunset.

For those seeking a more immersive cultural experience, Alegria offers plenty of opportunities to connect with the local community and learn about its rich heritage. Visit the town's historic church, a beautiful colonial-era building with ornate architecture and intricate wood carvings, or explore the nearby Mayan ruins of San Andrés, where you can glimpse into the region's ancient past.

As the sun sets over Alegria, casting a warm golden glow over its picturesque streets and rooftops, you'll find yourself reluctant to leave behind the magic of this charming town. But as you bid farewell to Alegria, you'll carry with you memories of laughter, friendship, and the indomitable spirit of a town that truly knows how to smile.

Joyful Journeys in Juayúa

Nestled amidst the verdant hills of western El Salvador, Juayúa beckons travellers with promises of joyful journeys and unforgettable experiences. This charming town, with its colourful streets and vibrant culture, is a hidden gem waiting to be discovered by adventurers seeking to immerse themselves in the heart and soul of Salvadoran life.

As you arrive in Juayúa, you'll be greeted by the sight of brightly painted buildings adorned with intricate murals, each telling a story of the town's rich history and cultural heritage. The air is filled with the tantalising aroma of street food sizzling on grills, drawing you in with promises of culinary delights waiting to be savoured.

Juayúa is perhaps best known for its famous food festival, held every weekend in the town's central plaza. Here, visitors can sample a mouth-watering array of traditional dishes, from hearty stews and grilled meats to fresh seafood and handmade tortillas. Take a seat at one of the bustling food stalls and feast on local favourites such as pupusas, tamales, and empanadas, all washed down with a glass of chilled horchata or tamarind juice – a true taste of Juayúa's culinary treasures.

But the town's delights extend beyond its gastronomic offerings. Juayúa is also a haven for art and culture, with galleries showcasing the work of local artists and artisans, and colourful street markets selling handmade crafts and souvenirs. Take a leisurely stroll through the town's winding streets, and you'll encounter vibrant murals, lively music, and friendly faces at every turn.

For those seeking outdoor adventures, Juayúa offers plenty of opportunities to explore the surrounding countryside and immerse yourself in the beauty of nature. Embark on a hike through the nearby coffee plantations, where you can learn about the region's rich coffee-growing heritage and sample freshly brewed beans straight from the source. Or venture into the nearby waterfalls and natural pools, where you can cool off with a refreshing swim in crystal-clear waters surrounded by lush tropical foliage.

As the sun sets over Juayúa, casting a warm glow over its picturesque streets and bustling plazas, you'll find yourself reluctant to leave behind the magic of this enchanting town. But as you bid farewell to Juayúa, you'll carry with you memories of joyful journeys, delicious food, and the warm hospitality of a community that welcomes travellers with open arms and open hearts.

El Espino: Beach Bliss and Seafood Delights

Nestled along the sun-kissed shores of El Salvador's Pacific coast, El Espino emerges as a tranquil haven for beach lovers and seafood enthusiasts alike. This idyllic coastal village, with its pristine beaches and mouth-watering culinary offerings, invites travellers to unwind in the lap of seaside luxury and indulge in the simple pleasures of life by the sea.

As you approach El Espino, you'll be greeted by the sight of palm-fringed beaches stretching as far as the eye can see, their golden sands inviting you to kick off your shoes and feel the warm embrace of the sun on your skin. The rhythmic sound of waves crashing against the shore creates a soothing soundtrack that instantly puts you at ease, washing away the stresses of everyday life and inviting you to embrace the laid-back pace of coastal living.

El Espino is renowned for its delectable seafood, freshly caught from the bountiful waters of the Pacific Ocean. Take a stroll along the beachfront promenade, where you'll find a plethora of charming seafood shacks and open-air restaurants serving up a tantalising array of culinary delights. Feast on succulent grilled fish, plump shrimp, and tender octopus, all seasoned to perfection with local spices and herbs, and washed down with a cold beer or a refreshing cocktail – a true taste of El Espino's coastal bounty.

But El Espino offers more than just sun, sand, and seafood – it's also a paradise for outdoor enthusiasts and nature lovers. Embark on a leisurely stroll along the beach, where you can explore hidden coves, collect seashells, and bask in the warm glow of the setting sun. Or venture into the nearby mangrove forests and nature reserves, where you can kayak through winding waterways, spot exotic bird species, and immerse yourself in the tranquillity of untouched wilderness.

For those seeking adventure, El Espino offers plenty of opportunities for surfing, snorkelling, and diving, with pristine waves and vibrant coral reefs just waiting to be explored. Whether you're a seasoned pro or a first-time visitor, the waters of El Espino beckon with promises of thrilling experiences and unforgettable memories.

As the sun dips below the horizon, casting a golden glow over the tranquil waters of the Pacific, you'll find yourself reluctant to leave behind the blissful shores of El Espino. But as you bid farewell to this coastal paradise, you'll carry with you memories of sun-drenched days, star-filled nights, and the timeless allure of life by the sea.

Afterword

As we come to the close of our journey through the vibrant landscapes and rich culture of El Salvador, it's time to reflect on the experiences we've shared and the memories we've made along the way. From the bustling streets of San Salvador to the tranquil beaches of El Espino, our travels have taken us on a whirlwind adventure through this captivating country, uncovering hidden treasures and forging unforgettable connections with its people.

El Salvador, with its diverse landscapes and warm hospitality, offers something for every traveller, whether you're seeking outdoor adventures, cultural experiences, or simply a chance to relax and unwind in paradise. From the rugged beauty of its national parks to the colonial charm of its historic towns, each destination has its own unique story to tell and its own magic to share with those who are willing to explore.

But perhaps the true beauty of El Salvador lies not just in its stunning scenery or delicious cuisine, but in the warmth and resilience of its people. Throughout our journey, we've been welcomed with open arms and treated to countless acts of kindness and generosity, reminding us that the true heart of any destination lies in the spirit of its inhabitants.

As we bid farewell to El Salvador, let us carry with us the memories of our adventures, the friendships we've forged, and the lessons we've learned along the way. May our experiences here inspire us to seek out new horizons, embrace new cultures, and continue our journey of discovery wherever it may lead.

So until we meet again, whether on the shores of El Espino or in the bustling streets of San Salvador, let us cherish the memories we've made and look forward to the adventures that lie ahead. As the sun sets on our time in El Salvador, let us carry with us the warmth of its people, the beauty of its landscapes, and the joy of our shared experiences, knowing that our journey here will live on in our hearts forever.

Printed in Great Britain
by Amazon